Songs of a
SOURDOUGH

Robert Service

A & C Black
London

Reprinted 2006
Reissued 2001
A & C Black Publishers Limited
38 Soho Square
London W1D 3HB
www.acblack.com

ISBN-10: 0-7136-5081-8
ISBN-13: 9-780-7136-5081-5

This edition first published in Great Britain 1957
by Ernest Benn Limited

A CIP catalogue record for this book is available from the British Library.

A & C Black uses paper produced with elemental chlorine-free pulp, harvested from
managed sustainable forests

Printed and bound in Great Britain by
The Cromwell Press,
Trowbridge, Wiltshire

CONTENTS

THE LAW OF THE YUKON	9
THE PARSON'S SON	17
THE SPELL OF THE YUKON	22
THE CALL OF THE WILD	26
THE LONE TRAIL	30
THE HEART OF THE SOURDOUGH	33
THE THREE VOICES	36
THE PINES	38
THE HARPY	42
THE LURE OF LITTLE VOICES	47
THE SONG OF THE WAGE-SLAVE	50
GRIN	54
THE SHOOTING OF DAN MCGREW	57
THE CREMATION OF SAM MCGEE	64
MY MADONNA	71
UNFORGOTTEN	73
THE RECKONING	74
QUATRAINS	76
THE MEN THAT DON'T FIT IN	79
MUSIC IN THE BUSH	81
THE RHYME OF THE REMITTANCE MAN	85
THE LOW-DOWN WHITE	89
THE LITTLE OLD LOG CABIN	92
THE YOUNGER SON	95
THE MARCH OF THE DEAD	99
"FIGHTING MAC"	103
THE WOMAN AND THE ANGEL	107
THE RHYME OF THE RESTLESS ONES	110
NEW YEAR'S EVE	113
COMFORT	118
PREMONITION	120
THE TRAMPS	122
L'ENVOI	124

To
C.M.

The lonely sunsets flare forlorn
  Down valleys dreadly desolate :
The lordly mountains soar in scorn,
  As still as death, as stern as fate.

      The lonely sunsets flame and die ;
        The giant valleys gulp the night ;
      The monster mountains scrape the sky,
        Where eager stars are diamond-bright.

So gaunt against the gibbous moon,
  Piercing the silence velvet-piled,
A lone wolf howls his ancient rune,
  The fell arch-spirit of the Wild.

      O outcast land !   O leper land !
        Let the lone wolf-cry all express—
      The hate insensate of thy hand,
        Thy heart's abysmal loneliness.

THE LAW OF THE YUKON

THIS is the law of the Yukon, and ever she makes
it plain:

"Send not your foolish and feeble; send me your
strong and your sane.

Strong for the red rage of battle; sane, for I
harry them sore;

Send me men girt for the combat, men who are
grit to the core;

Swift as the panther in triumph, fierce as the bear
in defeat,

Sired of a bulldog parent, steeled in the furnace
heat.

Send me the best of your breeding, lend me your
chosen ones;

9

Them will I take to my bosom, them will I call
  my sons;

Them will I gild with my treasure, them will I
  glut with my meat;

But the others—the misfits, the failures—I trample
  under my feet.

Dissolute, damned, and despairful, crippled and
  palsied and slain,

Ye would send me the spawn of your gutters—
  Go! take back your spawn again."

"Wild and wide are my borders, stern as death is
  my sway;

From my ruthless throne I have ruled alone for
  a million years and a day;

Hugging my mighty treasure, waiting for man to
  come:

Till he swept like a turbid torrent, and after him
  swept—the scum.

The pallid pimp of the dead-line, the enervate of
  the pen,

One by one I weeded them out, for all that I
  sought was—Men.

One by one I dismayed them, frighting them sore
  with my glooms;

One by one I betrayed them unto my manifold
  dooms.

Drowned them like rats in my rivers, starved them
  like curs on my plains,

Rotted the flesh that was left them, poisoned the
  blood in their veins;

Burst with my winter upon them, searing forever
  their sight,

Lashed them with fungus-white faces, whimpering
  wild in the night;

Staggering blind through the storm-whirl, stumb-
  ling mad through the snow,

Frozen stiff in the ice pack, brittle and bent like
  a bow;

Featureless, formless, forsaken, scented by wolves
  in their flight,

Left for the wind to make music through ribs that
  are glittering white;

Gnawing the black crust of failure, searching the
    pit of despair,

Crooking the toe in the trigger, trying to patter
    a prayer;

Going outside with an escort, raving with lips all
    afoam;

Writing a cheque for a million, drivelling feebly
    of home;

Lost like a louse in the burning . . . or else in
    tented town

Seeking a drunkard's solace, sinking and sinking
    down;

Steeped in the slime at the bottom, dead to a
    decent world,

Lost 'mid the human flotsam, far on the frontier
    hurled;

In the camp at the bend of the river, with its dozen
    saloons aglare,

Its gambling dens a-riot, its gramophones all
    a-blare;

Crimped with the crimes of a city, sin-ridden and
    bridled with lies,

In the hush of my mountained vastness, in the
    flush of my midnight skies.

Plague-spots, yet tools of my purpose, so natheless
    I suffer them thrive,

Crushing my Weak in their clutches, that only my
    Strong may survive."

"But the others, the men of my mettle, the men
    who would 'stablish my fame,

Unto its ultimate issue, winning me honour, not
    shame;

Searching my uttermost valleys, fighting each step
    as they go,

Shooting the wrath of my rapids, scaling my
    ramparts of snow;

Ripping the guts of my mountains, looting the beds
    of my creeks,

Them will I take to my bosom, and speak as a
    mother speaks.

I am the land that listens, I am the land that
    broods;

Steeped in eternal beauty, crystalline waters and
    woods.

Long have I waited lonely, shunned as a thing
    accurst,

Monstrous, moody, pathetic, the last of the lands
    and the first;

Visioning camp-fires at twilight, sad with a longing
    forlorn,

Feeling my womb o'er-pregnant with the seed of
    cities unborn.

Wild and wide are my borders, stern as death is
    my sway,

And I wait for the men who will win me—and I
    will not be won in a day;

And I will not be won by weaklings, subtile, suave,
    and mild,

But by men with the hearts of vikings, and the
    simple faith of a child;

Desperate, strong, and resistless, unthrottled by
    fear or defeat,

Them will I gild with my treasure, them will I
    glut with my meat."

"Lofty I stand from each sister land, patient and
wearily wise,

With the weight of a world of sadness in my quiet,
passionless eyes;

Dreaming alone of a people, dreaming alone of
a day,

When men shall not rape my riches, and curse me
and go away;

Making a bawd of my bounty, fouling the hand
that gave—

Till I rise in my wrath and I sweep on their path
and I stamp them into a grave.

Dreaming of men who will bless me, of women
esteeming me good,

Of children born in my borders, of radiant mother-
hood;

Of cities leaping to stature, of fame like a flag
unfurled,

As I pour the tide of my riches in the eager lap
of the world."

This is the Law of the Yukon, that only the Strong
    shall thrive;

That surely the Weak shall perish, and only the
    Fit survive.

Dissolute, damned, and despairful, crippled and
    palsied and slain,

This is the Will of the Yukon,—Lo! how she
    makes it plain.

THE PARSON'S SON

*THIS is the song of the parson's son, as he squats in
    his shack alone,*

*On the wild, weird nights when the Northern Lights
    shoot up from the frozen zone,*

*And it's sixty below, and couched in the snow the hungry
    huskies moan.*

"I'm one of the Arctic brotherhood, I'm an old-
    time pioneer.

I came with the first—O God! how I've cursed
    this Yukon—but still I'm here.

I've sweated athirst in its summer heat, I've
    frozen and starved in its cold;

I've followed my dreams by its thousand streams,
    I've toiled and moiled for its gold."

"Look at my eyes—been snow-blind twice; look
where my foot's half gone;
And that gruesome scar on my left cheek where
the frost-fiend bit to the bone.
Each one a brand of this devil's land, where I've
played and I've lost the game,
A broken wreck with a craze for 'hooch,' and
never a cent to my name."

"This mining is only a gamble, the worst is as
good as the best;
I was in with the bunch and I might have come
out right on top with the rest;
With Cormack, Ladue and Macdonald—O God!
but it's hell to think
Of the thousands and thousands I've squandered
on cards and women and drink."

"In the early days we were just a few, and we
hunted and fished around,
Nor dreamt by our lonely camp-fires of the wealth
that lay under the ground.

We traded in skins and whiskey, and I've often
    slept under the shade
Of that lone birch tree on Bonanza, where the first
    big find was made."

"We were just like a great big family, and every
    man had his squaw,
And we lived such a wild, free, fearless life beyond
    the pale of the law;
Till sudden there came a whisper, and it maddened
    us every man,
And I got in on Bonanza before the big rush
    began."

"Oh, those Dawson days, and the sin and the blaze,
    and the town all open wide!
(If God made me in His likeness, sure He let the
    devil inside.)
But we all were mad, both the good and the bad,
    and as for the women, well—
No spot on the map in so short a space has hustled
    more souls to hell."

"Money was just like dirt there, easy to get and
to spend.

I was all caked in on a dance-hall jade, but she
shook me in the end.

It put me queer, and for near a year I never drew
sober breath,

Till I found myself in the bughouse ward with a
claim staked out on death."

"Twenty years in the Yukon, struggling along its
creeks;

Roaming its giant valleys, scaling its god-like
peaks;

Bathed in its fiery sunsets, fighting its fiendish
cold,

Twenty years in the Yukon . . . twenty years—
and I'm old."

"Old and weak, but no matter, there's 'hooch' in
the bottle still.

I'll hitch up the dogs to-morrow, and mush down
the trail to Bill.

It's so long dark, and I'm lonesome—I'll just lay
down on the bed,
To-morrow I'll go . . . to-morrow . . . I guess I'll
play on the red."

" . . . Come, Kit, your pony is saddled. I'm
waiting, dear, in the court . . .

. . . Minnie, you devil, I'll kill you if you skip
with that flossy sport . . .

. . . How much does it go to the pan, Bill? . . .
play up, School, and play the game . . .

. . . Our Father, which art in heaven, hallowed be
Thy name . . ."

*This was the song of the parson's son, as he lay in
his bunk alone,*

*Ere the fire went out and the cold crept in, and his
blue lips ceased to moan,*

*And the hunger-maddened malamutes had torn him
flesh from bone.*

THE SPELL OF THE YUKON

I WANTED the gold, and I sought it;
  I scrabbled and mucked like a slave.
Was it famine or scurvy—I fought it,
  I hurled my youth into the grave.
I wanted the gold and I got it—
  Came out with a fortune last fall,—
Yet somehow life's not what I thought it,
  And somehow the gold isn't all.

No! There's the land. (Have you seen it?)
  It's the cussedest land that I know,
From the big, dizzy mountains that screen it,
  To the deep, deathlike valleys below.
Some say God was tired when He made it;
  Some say it's a fine land to shun;
Maybe: but there's some as would trade
  For no land on earth—and I'm one.

You come to get rich (damned good reason),
  You feel like an exile at first;
You hate it like hell for a season,
  And then you are worse than the worst.
It grips you like some kinds of sinning;
  It twists you from foe to a friend;
It seems it's been since the beginning;
  It seems it will be to the end.

I've stood in some mighty-mouthed hollow
  That's plumb-full of hush to the brim;
I've watched the big, husky sun wallow
  In crimson and gold, and grow dim,
Till the moon set the pearly peaks gleaming,
  And the stars tumbled out, neck and crop;
And I've thought that I surely was dreaming,
  With the peace o' the world piled on top.

The summer—no sweeter was ever;
  The sunshiny woods all athrill;
The greyling aleap in the river,
  The bighorn asleep on the hill.

The strong life that never knows harness;
  The wilds where the caribou call;
The freshness, the freedom, the farness—
  O God! how I'm stuck on it all.

The winter! the brightness that blinds you,
  The white land locked tight as a drum,
The cold fear that follows and finds you,
  The silence that bludgeons you dumb.
The snows that are older than history,
  The woods where the weird shadows slant;
The stillness, the moonlight, the mystery,
  I've bade 'em good-bye—but I can't.

There's a land where the mountains are nameless,
  And the rivers all run God knows where;
There are lives that are erring and aimless,
  And deaths that just hang by a hair;
There are hardships that nobody reckons;
  There are valleys unpeopled and still;
There's a land—oh, it beckons and beckons,
  And I want to go back—and I will.

They're making my money diminish;
  I'm sick of the taste of champagne.
Thank God! when I'm skinned to a finish
  I'll pike to the Yukon again.
I'll fight—and you bet it's no sham-fight;
  It's hell!—but I've been there before;
And it's better than this by a damsite—
  So me for the Yukon once more.

There's gold, and it's haunting and haunting,
  It's luring me on as of old;
Yet it isn't the gold that I'm wanting
  So much as just finding the gold.
It's the great, big, broad land 'way up yonder,
  It's the forests where silence has lease;
It's the beauty that thrills me with wonder,
  It's the stillness that fills me with peace.

THE CALL OF THE WILD

Have you gazed on naked grandeur where there's
      nothing else to gaze on,
  Set pieces and drop-curtain scenes galore,
Big mountains heaved to heaven, which the blind-
      ing sunsets blazon,
  Black canyons where the rapids rip and roar?
Have you swept the visioned valley with the green
      stream streaking through it,
  Searched the Vastness for a something you have
      lost?
Have you strung your soul to silence? Then for
      God's sake go and do it;
  Hear the challenge, learn the lesson, pay the cost.

Have you wandered in the wilderness, the sage-
      brush desolation,
  The bunch-grass levels where the cattle graze?

26

Have you whistled bits of rag-time at the end of
　　all creation,

　And learned to know the desert's little ways?

Have you camped upon the foothills, have you
　　galloped o'er the ranges,

　Have you roamed the arid sun-lands through
　　and through?

Have you chummed up with the mesa? Do you
　　know its moods and changes?

　Then listen to the wild—it's calling you.

Have you known the Great White Silence, not a
　　snow-gemmed twig a-quiver?

　(Eternal truths that shame our soothing lies.)

Have you broken trail on snowshoes? Mushed your
　　huskies up the river,

　Dared the unknown, led the way, and clutched
　　the prize?

Have you marked the map's void spaces, mingled
　　with the mongrel races,

　Felt the savage strength of brute in every
　　thew?

And though grim as hell the worst is, can you
　　　round it off with curses?
　　Then hearken to the wild—it's wanting you.

Have you suffered, starved, and triumphed,
　　　grovelled down, yet grasped at glory,
　　Grown bigger in the bigness of the whole?
"Done things" just for the doing, letting babblers
　　　tell the story.
　　　Seeing through the nice veneer the naked
　　　　soul?
Have you seen God in His splendours, heard the
　　　text that nature renders?
　　(You'll never hear it in the family pew.)
The simple things, the true things, the silent men
　　　who do things—
　　Then listen to the wild—it's calling you.

They have cradled you in custom, they have
　　　primed you with their preaching,
　　They have soaked you in convention through
　　　and through;

They have put you in a showcase; you're a credit
      to their teaching—

  But can't you hear the wild—it's calling you.

Let us probe the silent places, let us seek what
      luck betide us;

  Let us journey to a lonely land I know,

There's a whisper on the night-wind, there's a star
      agleam to guide us,

  And the wild is calling, calling . . . let us go.

THE LONE TRAIL

YE who know the Lone Trail fain would follow it,
Though it lead to glory or the darkness of the pit.
Ye who take the Lone Trail, bid your love good-bye;
The Lone Trail, the Lone Trail follow till you die.

The trails of the world be countless, and most of
the trails be tried;

You tread on the heels of the many, till you come
where the ways divide;

And one lies safe in the sunlight, and the other
is dreary and wan,

Yet you look aslant at the Lone Trail, and the
Lone Trail lures you on.

And somehow you're sick of the highway, with
its noise and its easy needs,

And you seek the risk of the by-way, and you reck
not where it leads.

And sometimes it leads to the desert, and the
tongue swells out of the mouth,

And you stagger blind to the mirage, to die in the
mocking drouth.

And sometimes it leads to the mountain, to the
light of the lone camp-fire,

And you gnaw your belt in the anguish of hunger-
goaded desire.

And sometimes it leads to the Southland, to the
swamp where the orchid glows,

And you rave to your grave with the fever, and
they rob the corpse for its clothes.

And sometimes it leads to the Northland, and the
scurvy softens your bones,

And your flesh dints in like putty, and you spit
out your teeth like stones.

And sometimes it leads to a coral reef in the wash
of a weedy sea,

And you sit and stare at the empty glare where
the gulls wait greedily.

And sometimes it leads to an Arctic trail, and the
snows where your torn feet freeze,

And you whittle away the useless clay, and crawl
    on your hands and knees.
Often it leads to the dead-pit; always it leads to
    pain;
By the bones of your brothers ye know it, but oh,
    to follow you're fain.
By your bones they will follow behind you, till the
    ways of the world are made plain.

Bid good-bye to sweetheart, bid good-bye to friend;
The Lone Trail, the Lone Trail follow to the end.
Tarry not, and fear not, chosen of the true;
Lover of the Lone Trail, the Lone Trail waits for you.

THE HEART OF THE SOURDOUGH

There where the mighty mountains bare their
    fangs unto the moon;
There where the sullen sun-dogs glare in the snow-
    bright, bitter noon,
And the glacier-gutted streams sweep down at the
    clarion call of June:

There where the livid tundras keep their tryst with
    the tranquil snows;
There where the Silences are spawned, and the
    light of hell-fire flows
Into the bowl of the midnight sky, violet, amber,
    and rose:

There where the rapids churn and roar, and the
    ice-floes bellowing run;

Where the tortured, twisted rivers of blood rush
    to the setting sun—
I've packed my kit and I'm going, boys, ere
    another day is gone.

.   .   .   .   .   .

I knew it would call, or soon or late, as it calls
    the whirring wings;
It's the olden lure, it's the golden lure, it's the
    lure of the timeless things;
And to-night, O God of the trails untrod, how
    it whines in my heart-strings!

I'm sick to death of your well-groomed gods, your
    make-believe and your show;
I long for a whiff of bacon and beans, a snug
    shake-down in the snow,
A trail to break, and a life at stake, and another
    bout with the foe;

With the raw-ribbed Wild that abhors all life,
    the Wild that would crush and rend;

I have clinched and closed with the naked North,
    I have learned to defy and defend;
Shoulder to shoulder we've fought it out—yet the
    Wild must win in the end.

I have flouted the Wild. I have followed its lure,
    fearless, familiar, alone;
By all that the battle means and makes I claim
    that land for mine own;
Yet the Wild must win, and a day will come
    when I shall be overthrown.

Then when as wolf-dogs fight we've fought, the
    lean wolf-land and I;
Fought and bled till the snows are red under the
    reeling sky;
Even as lean wolf-dog goes down will I go down
    and die.

THE THREE VOICES

THE waves have a story to tell me,
  As I lie on the lonely beach;
Chanting aloft in the pine-tops,
  The wind has a lesson to teach;
But the stars sing an anthem of glory
  I cannot put into speech.

The waves tell of ocean spaces,
  Of hearts that are wild and brave,
Of populous city places,
  Of desolate shores they lave;
Of men who sally in quest of gold
  To sink in an ocean grave.

The wind is a mighty roamer;
  He bids me keep me free,

Clean from the taint of the gold-lust,
  Hardy and pure as he;
Cling with my love to nature
  As a child to the mother knee.

But the stars throng out in their glory,
  And they sing of the God in man;
They sing of the mighty Master,
  Of the loom His fingers span;
Where a star or a soul is a part of the whole,
  And weft in the wondrous plan.

Here by the camp-fire's flicker,
  Deep in my blanket curled,
I long for the peace of the pine-gloom
  When the scroll of the Lord is unfurled,
And the wind and the wave are silent,
  And world is singing to world.

THE PINES

We sleep in the sleep of ages, the bleak, barbarian
    pines;
The grey moss drapes us like sages, and closer
    we lock our lines,
And deeper we clutch through the gelid gloom
    where never a sunbeam shines.

On the flanks of the storm-gored ridges are our
    black battalions massed;
We surge in a host to the sullen coast, and we
    sing in the ocean blast;
From empire of sea to empire of snow we grip
    our empire fast.

38

To the niggard lands were we driven, 'twixt
    desert and foe are we penned.

To us was the Northland given, ours to strong-
    hold and defend;

Ours till the world be riven in the crash of the
    utter end.

Ours from the bleak beginning, through the æons
    of death-like sleep;

Ours from the shock when the naked rock was
    hurled from the hissing deep;

Ours through the twilight ages of weary glacier-
    creep.

Wind of the East, wind of the West, wandering
    to and fro,

Chant your songs in our topmost boughs, that the
    sons of men may know

The peerless pine was the first to come, and the
    pine will be last to go!

We pillar the halls of perfumed gloom; we plume
    where the eagles soar;
The North-wind swoops from the brooding Pole,
    and our ancients crash and roar;
But where one falls from the crumbling walls
    shoots up a hardy score.

We spring from the gloom of the canyon's womb;
    in the valley's lap we lie;
From the white foam-fringe where the breakers
    cringe to the peaks that tusk the sky
We climb, and we peer in the crag-locked mere
    that gleams like a golden eye,—

Gain to the verge of the hog-back ridge where
    the vision ranges free:
Pines and pines and the shadow of pines as far
    as the eye can see;
A steadfast legion of stalwart knights in dominant
    empery.

Sun, moon and stars, give answer; shall we not
    staunchly stand
Even as now, forever, wards of the wilder strand,
Sentinels of the stillness, lords of the last lone
    land!

THE HARPY

*THERE was a woman, and she was wise; woefully
wise was she;*

*She was old, so old, yet her years all told were but a
score and three;*

*And she knew by heart, from finish to start, the Book
of Iniquity.*

There is no hope for such as I, on earth nor yet
in Heaven;

Unloved I live, unloved I die, unpitied, un-
forgiven;

A loathèd jade I ply my trade, unhallowed and
unshriven.

42

I paint my cheeks, for they are white, and cheeks
    of chalk men hate;

Mine eyes with wine I make to shine, that men
    may seek and sate;

With overhead a lamp of red I sit me down and
    wait.

Until they come, the nightly scum, with drunken
    eyes aflame;

Your sweethearts, sons, ye scornful ones—'tis I
    who know their shame;

The gods ye see are brutes to me—and so I play
    my game.

For life is not the thing we thought, and not the
    thing we plan;

And woman in a bitter world must do the best
    she can;

Must yield the stroke, and bear the yoke, and serve
    the will of man;

Must serve his need and ever feed the flame of
    his desire;
Though be she loved for love alone, or be she
    loved for hire;
For every man since life began is tainted with
    the mire.

And though you know he loves you so, and set
    you on love's throne,
Yet let your eyes but mock his sighs, and let your
    heart be stone,
Lest you be left (as I was left) attainted and
    alone.

From love's close kiss to hell's abyss is one sheer
    flight, I trow;
And wedding-ring and bridal bell are will-o'-wisps
    of woe;
And 'tis not wise to love too well, and this all
    women know.

Wherefore, the wolf-pack having gorged upon the
    lamb, their prey,
With siren smile and serpent guile I make the wolf-
    pack pay;
With velvet paws and flensing claws, a tigress
    roused to slay.

One who in youth sought truest truth, and found a
    devil's lies;
A symbol of the sin of man, a human sacrifice:
Yet shall I blame on man the shame? Could it
    be otherwise?

Was I not born to walk in scorn where others walk
    in pride?
The Maker marred, and evil-starred I drift upon
    His tide;
And He alone shall judge His own, so I His judg-
    ment bide.

*Fate has written a tragedy; its name is " The Human
    Heart."*

*The theatre is the House of Life, Woman the mummer's
    part :*

*The Devil enters the prompter's box and the play is ready
    to start.*

THE LURE OF LITTLE VOICES

THERE's a cry from out the Loneliness—Oh, listen,
     Honey, listen!
  Do you hear it, do you fear it, you're a-holding
     of me so?
You're a-sobbing in your sleep, dear, and your
     lashes, how they glisten—
  Do you hear the Little Voices all a-begging me
     to go?

All a-begging me to leave you. Day and night
     they're pleading, praying,
  On the North-wind, on the West-wind, from the
     peak and from the plain;
Night and day they never leave me—do you know
     what they are saying?
  "He was ours before you got him, and we want
     him once again."

Yes, they're wanting me, they're haunting me, the
    awful lonely places;
  They're whining and they're whimpering as if
    each had a soul;
They're calling from the wilderness, the vast and
    god-like spaces,
  The stark and sullen solitudes that sentinel the
    Pole.

They miss my little camp-fires, ever brightly,
    bravely gleaming
  In the womb of desolation where was never man
    before;
As comradeless I sought them, lion-hearted, loving,
    dreaming;
  And they hailed me as a comrade, and they loved
    me evermore.

And now they're all a-crying, and it's no use me
    denying:
  The spell of them is on me and I'm helpless as
    a child;

My heart is aching, aching, but I hear them sleep-
ing, waking;

  It's the Lure of Little Voices, it's the mandate
  of the Wild.

I'm afraid to tell you, Honey, I can take no bitter
leaving;

  But softly in the sleep-time from your love I'll
  steal away.

Oh, it's cruel, dearie, cruel, and it's God knows
how I'm grieving;

  But His Loneliness is calling and He knows I
  must obey.

THE SONG OF THE WAGE-SLAVE

WHEN the long, long day is over, and the Big Boss
gives me my pay,
I hope that it won't be hell-fire, as some of the
parsons say.
And I hope that it won't be heaven, with some of
the parsons I've met—
All I want is just quiet, just to rest and forget.
Look at my face, toil-furrowed; look at my
calloused hands;
Master, I've done Thy bidding, wrought in Thy
many lands—
Wrought for the little masters, big-bellied they be,
and rich;
I've done their desire for a daily hire, and I die
like a dog in a ditch.

I have used the strength Thou hast given, Thou
    knowest I did not shirk;

Threescore years of labour—Thine be the long
    day's work.

And now, Big Master, I'm broken and bent and
    twisted and scarred,

But I've held my job, and Thou knowest, and
    Thou wilt not judge me hard.

Thou knowest my sins are many, and often I've
    played the fool—

Whiskey and cards and women, they made me the
    devil's tool.

I was just like a child with money: I flung it away
    with a curse,

Feasting a fawning parasite, or glutting a harlot's
    purse,

Then back to the woods repentant, back to the
    mill or the mine,

I, the worker of workers, everything in my
    line.

Everything hard but headwork (I'd no more brains
    than a kid),

A brute with brute strength to labour, doing as I
    was bid;

Living in camps with men-folk, a lonely and love-
    less life;

Never knew kiss of sweetheart, never caress of
    wife.

A brute with brute strength to labour, and they
    were so far above—

Yet I'd gladly have gone to the gallows for one
    little look of Love.

I with the strength of two men, savage and shy
    and wild—

Yet how I'd ha' treasured a woman, and the
    sweet, warm kiss of a child.

Well, 'tis Thy world, and Thou knowest, I blas-
    pheme and my ways be rude;

But I've lived my life as I found it, and I've done
    my best to be good;

I, the primitive toiler, half naked, and grimed to
    the eyes,

Sweating it deep in their ditches, swining it stark
    in their styes.

Hurling down forests before me, spanning tumul-
tuous streams;

Down in the ditch building o'er me palaces fairer
than dreams;

Boring the rock to the ore-bed, driving the road
through the fen,

Resolute, dumb, uncomplaining, a man in a world
of men.

Master, I've filled my contract, wrought in Thy
many lands;

Not by my sins wilt Thou judge me, but by the
work of my hands.

Master, I've done Thy bidding, and the light is
low in the west,

And the long, long shift is over . . . Master, I've
earned it—Rest.

GRIN

I<small>F</small> you're up against a bruiser and you're getting
  knocked about—

>   Grin.

If you're feeling pretty groggy, and you're licked
  beyond a doubt—

>   Grin.

Don't let him see you're funking, let him know
  with every clout,

Though your face is battered to a pulp, your
  blooming heart is stout;

Just stand upon your pins until the beggar knocks
  you out—

>   And grin.

This life's a bally battle, and the same advice
  holds true,

>   Of grin.

54

If you're up against it badly, then it's only one
  on you,

So grin.

If the future's black as thunder, don't let people
  see you're blue;

Just cultivate a cast-iron smile of joy the whole
  day through;

If they call you "Little Sunshine," wish that *they'd*
  no troubles, too—

You may—grin.

Rise up in the morning with the will that, smooth
  or rough,

You'll grin.

Sink to sleep at midnight, and although you're
  feeling tough,

Yet grin.

There's nothing gained by whining, and you're not
  that kind of stuff;

You're a fighter from away back, and you *won't*
  take a rebuff:

Your trouble is that you don't know when you
    have had enough—

                    Don't give in.

If Fate should down you, just get up and take
    another cuff;

You may bank on it that there is no philosophy
    like bluff,

                    And grin.

THE SHOOTING OF DAN McGREW

A BUNCH of the boys were whooping it up in the
    Malamute saloon;

The kid that handles the music-box was hitting a
    jag-time tune;

Back of the bar, in a solo game, sat Dangerous
    Dan McGrew,

And watching his luck was his light-o'-love, the
    lady that's known as Lou.

When out of the night, which was fifty below,
    and into the din and the glare,

There stumbled a miner fresh from the creeks,
    dog-dirty and loaded for bear.

He looked like a man with a foot in the grave,
    and scarcely the strength of a louse,
Yet he tilted a poke of dust on the bar, and he
    called for drinks for the house.
There was none could place the stranger's face,
    though we searched ourselves for a clue;
But we drank his health, and the last to drink
    was Dangerous Dan McGrew.

There's men that somehow just grip your eyes,
    and hold them hard like a spell;
And such was he, and he looked to me like a
    man who had lived in hell;
With a face most hair, and the dreary stare of a
    dog whose day is done,
As he watered the green stuff in his glass, and
    the drops fell one by one.
Then I got to figgering who he was, and wondering
    what he'd do,
And I turned my head—and there watching him
    was the lady that's known as Lou.

His eyes went rubbering round the room, and he
    seemed in a kind of daze,
Till at last that old piano fell in the way of his
    wandering gaze.
The rag-time kid was having a drink; there was
    no one else on the stool,
So the stranger stumbles across the room, and
    flops down there like a fool.
In a buckskin shirt that was glazed with dirt he
    sat, and I saw him sway;
Then he clutched the keys with his talon hands—
    my God! but that man could play!

Were you ever out in the Great Alone, when the
    moon was awful clear,
And the icy mountains hemmed you in with a
    silence you most could *hear*;
With only the howl of a timber wolf, and you
    camped there in the cold,
A half-dead thing in a stark, dead world, clean
    made for the muck called gold;

While high overhead, green, yellow, and red, the
    North Lights swept in bars—
Then you've a hunch what the music meant . . .
    hunger and night and the stars.

And hunger not of the belly kind, that's banished
    with bacon and beans;
But the gnawing hunger of lonely men for a home
    and all that it means;
For a fireside far from the cares that are, four
    walls and a roof above;
But oh! so cramful of cosy joy, and crowned with
    a woman's love;
A woman dearer than all the world, and true as
    Heaven is true—
(God! how ghastly she looks through her rouge,—
    the lady that s known as Lou.)

Then on a sudden the music changed, so soft that
    you scarce could hear;
But you felt that your life had been looted clean
    of all that it once held dear;

That some-one had stolen the woman you loved;
    that her love was a devil's lie;
That your guts were gone, and the best for you
    was to crawl away and die.
'Twas the crowning cry of a heart's despair, and
    it thrilled you through and through—
"I guess I'll make it a spread misere," said Danger-
    ous Dan McGrew.

The music almost died away . . . then it burst
    like a pent-up flood;
And it seemed to say, "Repay, repay," and my
    eyes were blind with blood.
The thought came back of an ancient wrong, and
    it stung like a frozen lash,
And the lust awoke to kill, to kill . . . then the
    music stopped with a crash,

And the stranger turned, and his eyes they burned
    in a most peculiar way;
In a buckskin shirt that was glazed with dirt he
    sat, and I saw him sway;

Then his lips went in in a kind of grin, and he
    spoke, and his voice was calm;
And, "Boys," says he, "you don't know me, and
    none of you care a damn;
But I want to state, and my words are straight,
    and I'll bet my poke they're true,
That one of you is a hound of hell . . . and that
    one is Dan McGrew."

Then I ducked my head, and the lights went out,
    and two guns blazed in the dark;
And a woman screamed, and the lights went up,
    and two men lay stiff and stark;
Pitched on his head, and pumped full of lead, was
    Dangerous Dan McGrew,
While the man from the creeks lay clutched to the
    breast of the lady that's known as Lou.

These are the simple facts of the case, and I guess
    I ought to know;
They say that the stranger was crazed with
    "hooch," and I'm not denying it's so.

I'm not so wise as the lawyer guys, but strictly
    between us two—
The woman that kissed him and—pinched his
    poke—was the lady that's known as Lou.

THE CREMATION OF SAM McGEE

THERE *are* *strange* *things* *done* *in* *the* *midnight*
  sun
  By the men who moil for gold;
The Arctic trails have their secret tales
  That would make your blood run cold;
The Northern Lights have seen queer sights,
  But the queerest they ever did see
Was that night on the marge of Lake Lebarge
  I cremated Sam McGee.

Now Sam McGee was from Tennessee, where the
    cotton blooms and blows.
Why he left his home in the South to roam round
    the Pole God only knows.

He was always cold, but the land of gold seemed
    to hold him like a spell;
Though he'd often say in his homely way that
    he'd "sooner live in hell."

On a Christmas Day we were mushing our way
    over the Dawson trail.
Talk of your cold! through the parka's fold it
    stabbed like a driven nail.
If our eyes we'd close, then the lashes froze, till
    sometimes we couldn't see;
It wasn't much fun, but the only one to whimper
    was Sam McGee.

And that very night as we lay packed tight in our
    robes beneath the snow,
And the dogs were fed, and the stars o'erhead
    were dancing heel and toe,
He turned to me, and, "Cap," says he, "I'll cash
    in this trip, I guess;
And if I do, I'm asking that you won't refuse my
    last request."

Well, he seemed so low that I couldn't say no:
    then he says with a sort of moan:
"It's the cursèd cold, and it's got right hold till
    I'm chilled through to the bone.
Yet 'taint being dead, it's my awful dread of the
    icy grave that pains;
So I want you to swear that, foul or fair, you'll
    cremate my last remains."

A pal's last need is a thing to heed, so I swore I
    would not fail;
And we started on at the streak of dawn, but God!
    he looked ghastly pale.
He crouched on the sleigh, and he raved all day
    of his home in Tennessee;
And before nightfall a corpse was all that was left
    of Sam McGee.

There wasn't a breath in that land of death, and
    I hurried, horror driven,
With a corpse half-hid that I couldn't get rid
    because of a promise given;

It was lashed to the sleigh, and it seemed to say:
"You may tax your brawn and brains,
But you promised true, and it's up to you to
cremate those last remains."

Now a promise made is a debt unpaid, and the
trail has its own stern code.
In the days to come, though my lips were dumb,
in my heart how I cursed that load.
In the long, long night, by the lone firelight, while
the huskies, round in a ring,
Howled out their woes to the homeless snows—O
God! how I loathed the thing!

And every day that quiet clay seemed to heavy
and heavier grow;
And on I went, though the dogs were spent and
the grub was getting low;
The trail was bad, and I felt half mad, but I swore
I would not give in;
And I'd often sing to the hateful thing, and it
hearkened with a grin.

Till I came to the marge of Lake Lebarge, and a
    derelict there lay;
It was jammed in the ice, but I saw in a trice it
    was called the "Alice May."
And I looked at it, and I thought a bit, and I
    looked at my frozen chum:
Then, "Here," said I, with a sudden cry, "is my
    cre-ma-tor-eum."

Some planks I tore from the cabin floor, and I lit
    the boiler fire;
Some coal I found that was lying around, and I
    heaped the fuel higher;
The flames just soared, and the furnace roared—
    such a blaze you seldom see;
And I burrowed a hole in the glowing coal, and I
    stuffed in Sam McGee.
Then I made a hike, for I didn't like to hear him
    sizzle so;
And the heavens scowled, and the huskies howled,
    and the wind began to blow.

It was icy cold, but the hot sweat rolled down my
    cheeks, and I don't know why;

And the greasy smoke in an inky cloak went
    streaking down the sky.

I do not know how long in the snow I wrestled
    with grisly fear;

But the stars came out and they danced about ere
    again I ventured near;

I was sick with dread, but I bravely said: "I'll
    just take a peep inside.

I guess he's cooked, and it's time I looked," . . .
    then the door I opened wide.

And there sat Sam, looking cool and calm, in the
    heart of the furnace roar;

And he wore a smile you could see a mile, and he
    said: "Please close that door.

It's fine in here, but I greatly fear you'll let in the
    cold and storm—

Since I left Plumtree, down in Tennessee, it's the
    first time I've been warm."

There are strange things done in the midnight sun
  By the men who moil for gold ;
The Arctic trails have their secret tales
  That would make your blood run cold.
The Northern Lights have seen queer sights,
  But the queerest they ever did see
Was that night on the marge of Lake Lebarge
  I cremated Sam McGee.

MY MADONNA

I HALED me a woman from the street,
    Shameless, but, oh, so fair!
I bade her sit in the model's seat,
    And I painted her sitting there.

    I hid all trace of her heart unclean;
        I painted a babe at her breast;
    I painted her as she might have been
        If the Worst had been the Best.

She laughed at my picture, and went away.
    Then came, with a knowing nod,
A connoisseur, and I heard him say:
    "'Tis Mary, the Mother of God."

71

So I painted a halo round her hair,
　And I sold her, and took my fee,
And she hangs in the church of Saint Hilaire,
　Where you and all may see.

UNFORGOTTEN

I KNOW a garden where the lilies gleam,
  And one who lingers in the sunshine there;
  She is than white-stoled lily far more fair,
And oh, her eyes are heaven-lit with dream.

    I know a garret, cold and dark and drear,
        And one who toils and toils with tireless pen,
        Until his brave, sad eyes grow weary—then
    He seeks the stars, pale, silent as a seer.

And ah, it's strange, for desolate and dim
  Between these two there rolls an ocean wide;
  Yet he is in the garden by her side.
And she is in the garret there with him.

THE RECKONING

It's fine to have a blow-out in a fancy restaurant,
With terrapin and canvas-back and all the wine
    you want;
To enjoy the flowers and music, watch the pretty
    women pass,
Smoke a choice cigar, and sip the wealthy water
    in your glass;
It's bully in a high-toned joint to eat and drink
    your fill,
But it's quite another matter when you
                  Pay the bill.

It's great to go out every night on fun or pleasure
    bent,
To wear your glad rags always, and to never save
    a cent;

To drift along regardless, have a good time every
    trip;
To hit the high spots sometimes, and to let your
    chances slip;
To know you're acting foolish, yet to go on fooling
    still,
Till Nature calls a show-down, and you
                 Pay the bill.

Time has got a little bill—get wise while yet you
    may,
For the debit side's increasing in a most alarming
    way;
The things you had no right to do, the things you
    should have done,
They're all put down: it's up to you to pay for
    every one.
So eat, drink, and be merry, have a good time if
    you will,
But God help you when the time comes, and you
                 Foot the bill.

QUATRAINS

ONE said: Thy life is thine to make or mar,
To flicker feebly, or to soar, a star;
It lies with thee—the choice is thine, is thine,
To hit the ties or drive thy auto-car.

I answer Her: The choice is mine—ah, no!
We all were made or marred long, long ago.
The parts are written: hear the super wail:
"Who is stage-managing this cosmic show?"

Blind fools of fate, and slaves of circumstance,
Life is a fiddler, and we all must dance.
From gloom where mocks that will-o'-wisp, Free-
    will,
I heard a voice cry: "Say, give us a chance."

Chance! Oh, there is no chance. The scene is
    set.
Up with the curtain! Man, the marionette,
Resumes his part. The gods will work the wires.
They've got it all down fine, you bet, you bet!

It's all decreed: the mighty earthquake crash;
The countless constellations' wheel and flash;
The rise and fall of empires, war's red tide,
The composition of your dinner hash.

There's no haphazard in this world of ours:
Cause and effect are grim, relentless powers.
They rule the world. (A king was shot last
    night.
Last night I held the joker and both bowers.)

From out the mesh of fate our heads we thrust.
We can't do what we would, but what we must.
Heredity has got us in a cinch.
(Consoling thought, when you've been on a
    "bust.")

Hark to the song where spheral voices blend:
"There's no beginning, never will be end."
It makes us nutty; hang the astral chimes!
The table's spread; come, let us dine, my friend.

THE MEN THAT DON'T FIT IN

THERE's a race of men that don't fit in,
  A race that can't stay still;
So they break the hearts of kith and kin,
  And they roam the world at will.
They range the field and they rove the flood,
  And they climb the mountain's crest;
Theirs is the curse of the gipsy blood,
  And they don't know how to rest.

  If they just went straight they might go far;
    They are strong and brave and true;
  But they're always tired of the things that are,
    And they want the strange and new.
  They say: "Could I find my proper groove,
    What a deep mark I would make!"
  So they chop and change, and each fresh move
    Is only a fresh mistake.

79

And each forgets, as he strips and runs,
  With a brilliant, fitful pace,
It's the steady, quiet, plodding ones
  Who win in the lifelong race.
And each forgets that his youth has fled,
  Forgets that his prime is past,
Till he stands one day with a hope that's dead
  In the glare of the truth at last.

    He has failed, he has failed; he has missed
        his chance;
      He has just done things by half.
    Life's been a jolly good joke on him,
        And now is the time to laugh
    Ha, ha!   He is one of the Legion Lost;
      He was never meant to win;
    He's a rolling stone, and it's bred in the
        bone;
      He's a man who won't fit in.

MUSIC IN THE BUSH

O'ER the dark pines she sees the silver moon,
  And in the west, all tremulous, a star:
And soothing sweet she hears the mellow tune
  Of cow-bells jangled in the fields afar.

Quite listless, for her daily stint is done,
  She stands, sad exile, at her rose-wreathed door,
And sends her love eternal with the sun
  That goes to gild the land she'll see no more.

The grave, gaunt pines imprison her sad gaze.
  All still the sky and darkling drearily;
She feels the chilly breath of dear, dead day
  Come sifting through the alders eerily.

81

Oh, how the roses riot in their bloom!
  The curtains stir as with an ancient pain;
Her old piano gleams from out the gloom,
  And waits and waits her tender touch in vain.

But now her hands like moonlight brush the
      keys
  With velvet grace, melodious delight;
And now a sad refrain from overseas
  Goes sobbing on the bosom of the night.

And now she sings.   (O singer in the gloom,
  Voicing a sorrow we can ne'er express,
Here in the Farness where we few have room
  Unshamed to show our love and tenderness.

Our hearts will echo, till they beat no more,
  That song of sadness and of motherland;
And stretched in deathless love to England's
      shore,
  Some day she'll hearken and she'll understand.)

A prima-donna in the shining past,
  But now a mother growing old and grey,
She thinks of how she held a people fast
  In thrall, and gleaned the triumphs of a day.

She sees a sea of faces like a dream;
  She sees herself a queen of song once more;
She sees lips part in rapture, eyes agleam;
  She sings as never once she sang before.

She sings a wild, sweet song that throbs with
      pain,
  The added pain of life that transcends art,
A song of home, a deep, celestial strain,
  The glorious swan-song of a dying heart.

A lame tramp comes along the railway track,
  A grizzled dog whose day is nearly done:
He passes, pauses, then comes slowly back
  And listens there—an audience of one.

She sings—her golden voice is passion-fraught
  As when she charmed a thousand eager ears;
He listens trembling, and she knows it not,
  And down his hollow cheeks roll bitter tears.

She ceases and is still, as if to pray;
  There is no sound, the stars are all alight—
Only a wretch who stumbles on his way,
  Only a vagrant sobbing in the night.

THE RHYME OF THE REMITTANCE MAN

THERE'S a four-pronged buck a-swinging in the
      shadow of my cabin,
  And it roamed the velvet valley till to-day;
But I tracked it by the river, and I trailed it in
      the cover,
  And I killed it on the mountain miles away.
Now I've had my lazy supper, and the level sun
      is gleaming
  On the water where the silver salmon play;
And I light my little corn-cob, and I linger softly
      dreaming,
  In the twilight, of a land that's far away.

Far away, so faint and far, is flaming London,
      fevered Paris,
  That I fancy I have gained another star;

85

Far away the din and hurry, far away the sin and
worry,

Far away—God knows they cannot be too far.

Gilded galley-slaves of Mammon—how my purse-
proud brothers taunt me!

I might have been as well-to-do as they

Had I clutched like them my chances, learned
their wisdom, crushed my fancies,

Starved my soul and gone to business every
day.

Well, the cherry bends with blossom, and the
vivid grass is springing,

And the star-like lily nestles in the green;

And the frogs their joys are singing, and my heart
in tune is ringing.

And it doesn't matter what I might have
been.

While above the scented pine-gloom, piling heights
of golden glory,

The sun-god paints his canvas in the west:

I can couch me deep in clover, I can listen to
the story
Of the lazy, lapping water—it is best.

While the trout leaps in the river, and the blue
grouse thrills the cover,
And the frozen snow betrays the panther's
track,
And the robin greets the dayspring with the
rapture of a lover,
I am happy, and I'll nevermore go back.
For I know I'd just be longing for the little old
log cabin,
With the morning-glory clinging to the door,
Till I loathed the city places, cursed the care on
all the faces,
Turned my back on lazar London evermore.

So send me far from Lombard Street, and write
me down a failure;
Put a little in my purse and leave me free.

Say: "He turned from Fortune's offering to
      follow up a pale lure,
  He is one of us no longer—let him be."
I am one of you no longer; by the trails my feet
      have broken,
  The dizzy peaks I've scaled, the camp-fire's
      glow,
By the lonely seas I've sailed in—yea, the final
      word is spoken.
  I am signed and sealed to nature.   Be it so.

THE LOW-DOWN WHITE

This is the pay-day up at the mines, when the
    bearded brutes come down;
There's money to burn in the streets to-night, so
    I've sent my klooch to town,
With a haggard face and a ribband of red entwined
    in her hair of brown.

And I know at the dawn she'll come reeling home
    with the bottles, one, two, three;
One for herself to drown her shame, and two big
    bottles for me,
To make me forget the thing I am and the man
    I used to be.

To make me forget the brand of the dog, as I
    crouch in this hideous place;

To make me forget once I kindled the light of
    love in a lady's face,
Where even the squalid Siwash now holds me a
    black disgrace.

Oh, I have guarded my secret well! And who
    would dream as I speak
In a tribal tongue like a rogue unhung, 'mid the
    ranch-house filth and reek,
I could roll to bed with a Latin phrase, and rise
    with a verse of Greek?

Yet I was a senior prizeman once, and the pride
    of a college eight;
Called to the bar—my friends were true! but they
    could not keep me straight;
Then came the divorce, and I went abroad and
    "died" on the River Plate.

But I'm not dead yet; though with half a lung
    there isn't time to spare.

And I hope that the year will see me out, and,
    thank God, no one will care—
Save maybe the little slim Siwash girl with the
    rose of shame in her hair.

She will come with the dawn, and the dawn is
    near; I can see its evil glow,
Like a corpse-light seen through a frosty pane in
    a night of want and woe;
And yonder she comes, by the bleak bull-pines,
    swift staggering through the snow.

THE LITTLE OLD LOG CABIN

WHEN a man gits on his uppers in a hard-pan sort
of town,
An' he ain't got nothin' comin', an' he can't
afford ter eat.
An' he's in a fix fer lodgin', an' he wanders up
an' down,
An' you'd fancy he'd been boozin', he's so
locoed 'bout the feet;
When he's feelin' sneakin' sorry, an' his belt is
hangin' slack,
An' his face is peaked an' grey-like, an' his heart
gits down an' whines,
Then he's apt ter git a-thinkin' an' a-wishin' he
was back
In the little ol' log cabin in the shadder of the
pines.

When he's on the blazin' desert, an' his canteen's
    sprung a leak,
  An' he's all alone an' crazy, an' he's crawlin'
    like a snail,
An' his tongue's so black an' swollen that it hurts
    him fer to speak,
  An' he gouges down fer water, an' the raven's
    on his trail;
When he's done with care and cursin', an' he feels
    more like to cry,
  An' he sees ol' Death a-grinnin', an' he thinks
    upon his crimes,
Then he's like ter hev' a vision, as he settles down
    ter die,
  Of the little ol' log cabin an' the roses an' the
    vines.

Oh, the little ol' log cabin, it's a solemn shinin'
    mark
  When a feller gits ter sinnin', an' a-goin' ter
    the wall,

An' folks don't understand him, an' he's gropin' in
the dark,
An' he's sick of bein' cursed at, an' he's longin'
fer his call:
When the sun of life's a-sinkin' you can see it
'way above,
On the hill from out the shadder in a glory 'gin
the sky,
An' your mother's voice is callin', an' her arms
are stretched in love,
An' somehow you're glad you're goin', an' you
ain't a-scared to die;
When you'll be like a kid again, an' nestle to her
breast,
An' never leave its shelter, an' forget, an' love,
an' rest.

THE YOUNGER SON

IF you leave the gloom of London and you seek
    a glowing land,
  Where all except the flag is strange and
    new,
There's a bronzed and stalwart fellow who will
    grip you by the hand,
  And greet you with a welcome warm and
    true;
For he's your younger brother, the one you sent
    away,
  Because there wasn't room for him at home;
And now he's quite contented, and he's glad he
    didn't stay,
  And he's building Britains greatness o'er the
    foam.

When the giant herd is moving at the rising of
    the sun,
  And the prairie is lit with rose and gold;
And the camp is all a-bustle, and the busy day's
    begun,
  He leaps into the saddle sure and bold.
Through the round of heat and hurry, through the
    racket and the rout,
  He rattles at a pace that nothing mars;
And when the night-winds whisper, and camp-fires
    flicker out,
  He is sleeping like a child beneath the stars.

When the wattle-blooms are drooping in the
    sombre she-oak-glade,
  And the breathless land is lying in a swoon,
He leaves his work a moment, leaning lightly on
    his spade,
  And he hears the bell-bird chime the Austral
    noon.
The parakeets are silent in the gum-tree by the
    creek;
  The ferny grove is sunshine-steeped and still;

But the dew will gem the myrtle in the twilight
    ere he seek
  His little lonely cabin on the hill.

Around the purple, vine-clad slope the argent river
    dreams;
  The roses almost hide the house from view;
A snow-peak of the Winterberg in crimson splen-
    dour gleams;
  The shadow deepens down on the karroo
He seeks the lily-scented dusk beneath the orange
    tree:
  His pipe in silence glows and fades and
    glows,
And then two little maids come out and climb
    upon his knee,
  And one is like the lily, one the rose.

He sees his white sheep dapple o'er the green
    New Zealand plain,
  And where Vancouver's shaggy ramparts frown.

When the sunlight threads the pine-gloom he is
        fighting might and main
    To clinch the rivets of an Empire down.
You will find him toiling, toiling, in the south or
        in the west,
    A child of nature, fearless, frank and free:
And the warmest heart that beats for you is beating
        in his breast,
    And he sends you loyal greeting o'er the sea.

You've a brother in the Army, you've another in
        the Church;
    One of you is a diplomatic swell;
You've had the pick of everything and left him
        in the lurch;
    And yet I think he's doing very well.
I'm sure his life is happy, and he doesn't envy
        yours;
    I know he loves the land his pluck has won;
And I fancy in the years unborn, while England's
        fame endures,
    She will come to bless with pride—the Younger
        Son.

THE MARCH OF THE DEAD

THE cruel war was over—oh, the triumph was so
  sweet!
  We watched the troops returning, through our
    tears;
There was triumph, triumph, triumph down the
    scarlet glittering street,
  And you scarce could hear the music for the
    cheers.
And you scarce could see the house-tops for the
    flags that flew between,
  The bells were pealing madly to the sky;
And every one was shouting for the Soldiers of
    the Queen,
  And the glory of an age was passing by.

99

And then there came a shadow, swift and sudden,
    dark and drear;
  The bells were silent, not an echo stirred.
The flags were drooping sullenly, the men forgot
    to cheer;
  We waited, and we never spoke a word.
The sky grew darker, darker, till from out the
    gloomy rack
  There came a voice that checked the heart with
    dread:
"Tear down, tear down your bunting now, and
    hang up sable black;
  They are coming—it's the Army of the Dead."

They were coming, they were coming, gaunt and
    ghastly, sad and slow;
  They were coming, all the crimson wrecks of
    pride;
With faces scared, and cheeks red smeared, and
    haunting eyes of woe,
  And clotted holes the khaki couldn't hide.

Oh, the clammy brow of anguish! the livid, foam-
   flecked lips!

  The reeling ranks of ruin swept along!

The limb that trailed, the hand that failed, the
   bloody finger-tips!

  And oh, the dreary rhythm of their song!

"They left us on the veldt-side, but we felt we
   couldn't stop,

  On this, our England's crowning festal day;

We're the men of Magersfontein, we're the men of
   Spion Kop,

  Colenso,—we're the men who had to pay.

We're the men who paid the blood-price. Shall
   the grave be all our gain?

  You owe us.   Long and heavy is the score.

Then cheer us for our glory now, and cheer us for
   our pain,

  And cheer us as ye never cheered before."

The folks were white and stricken, and each tongue
   seemed weighed with lead;

  Each heart was clutched in hollow hand of ice;

And every eye was staring at the horror of the
    dead,

  The pity of the men who paid the price.

They were come, were come to mock us, in the
    first flush of our peace;

  Through writhing lips their teeth were all
    agleam;

They were coming in their thousands—oh, would
    they never cease!

  I closed my eyes, and then—it was a dream.

There was triumph, triumph, triumph down the
    scarlet gleaming street;

  The town was mad, a man was like a boy.

A thousand flags were flaming where the sky and
    city meet;

  A thousand bells were thundering the joy.

There was music, mirth and sunshine; but some
    eyes shone with regret:

  And while we stun with cheers our homing
    braves,

O God, in Thy great mercy, let us nevermore
    forget

  The graves they left behind, the bitter graves.

"FIGHTING MAC"

A LIFE TRAGEDY

A PISTOL-SHOT rings round and round the world:
  In pitiful defeat a warrior lies.
A last defiance to dark Death is hurled,
  A last wild challenge shocks the sunlit skies.
  Alone he falls with wide, wan, woeful eyes:
Eyes that could smile at death—could not face
    shame.

Alone, alone he paced his narrow room,
  In the bright sunshine of that Paris day;
Saw in his thought the awful hand of doom;
  Saw in his dream his glory pass away;
  Tried in his heart, his weary heart, to pray:
"O God! who made me, give me strength to face
The spectre of this bitter, black disgrace."

    .   .   .   .   .   .

103

The burn brawls darkly down the shaggy glen,
  The bee-kissed heather blooms around the door.
He sees himself a barefoot boy again,
  Bending o'er page of legendary lore.
  He hears the pibroch, grips the red claymore,
Runs with the Fiery Cross a clansman true,
Sworn kinsman of Rob Roy and Roderick Dhu.

Eating his heart out with a wild desire,
  One day, behind his counter trim and neat,
He hears a sound that sets his brain afire—
  The Highlanders are marching down the street.
  Oh, how the pipes shrill out, the mad drums
    beat!
"On to the gates of Hell, my Gordons gay!"
He flings his hated yardstick far away.

He sees the sullen pass, high-crowned with snow,
  Where Afghans cower with eyes of gleaming
    hate,
He hurls himself against the hidden foe.
  They try to rally—ah, too late, too late!
  Again, defenceless, with fierce eyes that wait

For death, he stands, like baited bull at bay,
And flouts the Boers, that mad Majuba day.

He sees again the murderous Soudan,
   Blood-slaked and rapine swept. He seems to
      stand
Upon the gory plain of Omdurman.
   Then Magersfontein, and supreme command
      Over his Highlanders. To shake his hand
A King is proud, and princes call him friend,
And glory crowns his life—and now the end.

The awful end. His eyes are dark with doom;
   He hears the shrapnel shrieking overhead:
He sees the ravaged ranks, the flame-stabbed
      gloom.
   Oh, to have fallen! the battle-field his bed,
   With Wauchope and his glorious brother-dead.
Why was he saved for this, for this? And now
He raises the revolver to his brow.

   .   .   .   .   .   .

In many a Highland home, framed with rude art,
  You'll find his portrait, rough-hewn, stern and
      square:
It's graven in the Fuyam fellah's heart;
  The Ghurka reads it at his evening prayer;
  The raw lands know it, where the fierce suns
      glare;
The Dervish fears it.   Honour to his name,
Who holds aloft the shield of England's fame.

Mourn for our hero, men of Northern race!
  We do not know his sin; we only know
His sword was keen.   He laughed death in the
      face,
  And struck, for Empire's sake, a giant blow.
  His arm was strong.   Ah! well they learnt, the
      foe.
The echo of his deeds is ringing yet,
Will ring for aye.   All else . . . let us forget.

THE WOMAN AND THE ANGEL

AN angel was tired of heaven, as he lounged in
    the golden street;

His halo was tilted sideways, and his harp lay mute
    at his feet;

So the Master stooped in His pity, and gave him
    a pass to go,

For the space of a moon, to the earth-world, to
    mix with the men below.

He doffed his celestial garments, scarce waiting
    to lay them straight;

He bade good-bye to Peter, who stood by the
    golden gate;

The sexless singers of heaven chanted a fond
    farewell,

And the imps looked up as they pattered on the
    red-hot flags of hell.

107

Never was seen such an angel; eyes of a heavenly
   blue,
Features that shamed Apollo, hair of a golden
   hue;
The women simply adored him, his lips were like
   Cupid's bow;
But he never ventured to use them—and so they
   voted him slow.

Till at last there came One Woman, a marvel of
   loveliness,
And she whispered to him: "Do you love me?"
   And he answered that woman, "Yes."
And she said: "Put your arms around me, and
   kiss me, and hold me—so—"
But fiercely he drew back, saying: "This thing is
   wrong, and I know."

Then sweetly she mocked his scruples, and softly
   she him beguiled:
"You, who are verily man among men, speak with
   the tongue of a child.

We have outlived the old standards; we have
    burst, like an over-tight thong,
The ancient, outworn, puritanic traditions of Right
    and Wrong."

Then the Master feared for His angel, and called
    him again to His side,
For oh, the woman was wondrous, and oh, the
    angel was tried,
And deep in his hell sang the Devil, and this was
    the strain of his song:
"The ancient, outworn, puritanic traditions of
    Right and Wrong."

THE RHYME OF THE RESTLESS ONES

We couldn't sit and study for the law;
  The stagnation of a bank we couldn't stand;
For our riot blood was surging, and we didn't need
      much urging
To excitements and excesses that are banned.
So we took to wine and drink and other things,
  And the devil in us struggled to be free;
Till our friends rose up in wrath, and they pointed
      out the path,
And they paid our debts and packed us o'er the
      sea.

Oh, they shook us off and shipped us o'er the
      foam,
To the larger lands that lure a man to roam;
        And we took the chance they gave
        Of a far and foreign grave,
And we bade goodbye for evermore to home.

And some of us are climbing on the peak,
   And some of us are camping on the plain;
By pine and palm you'll find us, with never claim
      to bind us,
By track and trail you'll meet us once again.

We are fated serfs to freedom—sky and sea;
   We have failed where slummy cities overflow;
But the stranger ways of earth know our pride and
      know our worth,
And we go into the dark as fighters go.

Yes, we go into the night as brave men go,
Though our faces they be often streaked with woe;
     Yet we're hard as cats to kill,
     And our hearts are reckless still
And we've danced with death a dozen times or so.

And you'll find us in Alaska after gold,
   And you'll find us herding cattle in the South.

We like strong drink and fun; and when the race
　　is run,
　We often die with curses in our mouth.

We are wild as colts unbroke, but never mean;
　Of our sins we've shoulders broad to bear the
　　blame;
But we'll never stay in town, and we'll never
　　settle down,
　And we'll never have an object or an aim.

No, there's that in us that time can never tame;
And life will always seem a careless game;
　　　And they'd better far forget—
　　　Those who say they love us yet—
Forget, blot out with bitterness our name.

NEW YEAR'S EVE

IT's cruel cold on the water-front, silent and dark
    and drear;
  Only the black tide weltering, only the hissing
    snow;
And I, alone, like a storm-tossed wreck, on this
    night of the glad New Year,
  Shuffling along in the icy wind, ghastly and
    gaunt and slow.

They're playing a tune in McGuffy's saloon, and
    it's cheery and bright in there
  (God! but I'm weak—since the bitter dawn, and
    never a bite of food);
I'll just go over and slip inside—I mustn't **give**
    way to despair—

Perhaps I can bum a little booze if the boys are
feeling good.

They'll jeer at me, and they'll sneer at me, and
they'll call me a whiskey soak;
("Have a drink? Well, thankee kindly, sir, I
don't mind if I do.")
A drivelling, dirty gin-joint fiend, the butt of the
bar-room joke;
Sunk and sodden and hopeless—"Another?
Well, here's to you!"

McGuffy is showing a bunch of the boys how Bob
Fitzsimmons hit;
The barman is talking of Tammany Hall, and
why the ward boss got fired;
I'll just sneak into a corner, and they'll let me
alone a bit;
The room is reeling round and round . . . O
God, but I'm tired, I'm tired. . . .

.   .   .   .   .   .

Roses she wore on her breast that night. Oh, but
    their scent was sweet;
  Alone we sat on the balcony, and the fan-palms
    arched above;
The witching strain of a waltz by Strauss came
    up to our cool retreat,
  And I prisoned her little hand in mine, and I
    whispered my plea of love.

Then sudden the laughter died on her lips, and
    lowly she bent her head;
  And oh, there came in the deep, dark eyes a
    look that was heaven to see,
And the moments went, and I waited there, and
    never a word was said,
  And she plucked from her bosom a rose of red,
    and shyly gave it to me.

Then the music swelled to a crash of joy, and the
    lights blazed up like day;
  And I held her fast to my throbbing heart, and
    I kissed her bonny brow;

"She is mine, she is mine for evermore!" the
    violins seemed to say.
  And the bells were ringing the New Year in—
    O God! I can hear them now.

Don't you remember that long, last waltz, with its
    sobbing, sad refrain?
  Don't you remember that last goodbye, and the
    dear eyes dim with tears?
Don't you remember that golden dream, with
    never a hint of pain,
  Of lives that would blend like an angel-song in
    the bliss of the coming year?

Oh, what have I lost! What have I lost! Ethel,
    forgive, forgive!
  The red, red rose is faded now, and it's fifty
    years ago.
Twere better to die a thousand deaths than live
    each day as I live!
  I have sinned, I have sunk to the lowest depths
    —but oh, I have suffered so!

Hark! Oh hark! I can hear the bells! . . .
    Look! I can see her there,
  Fair as a dream . . . but it fades . . . And now
    —I can hear the dreadful hum
Of the crowded court . . . See! the Judge looks
    down . . . Not Guilty, my Lord, I swear. . .
  The bells, I can hear the bells again . . . Ethel,
    I come, I come! . . .

    .   .   .   .   .   .

"Rouse up, old man, it's twelve o'clock. You
    can't sleep here, you know.
  Say! ain't you got no sentiment? Lift up your
    muddled head;
Have a drink to the glad New Year, a drop before
    you go—
  You darned old dirty hobo . . . My God!
    Here, boys! He's DEAD!"

COMFORT

SAY! You've struck a heap of trouble—
  Bust in business, lost your wife;
No one cares a cent about you,
  You don't care a cent for life;
Hard luck has of hope bereft you,
  Health is failing, wish you'd die—
Why, you've still the sunshine left you,
  And the big, blue sky.

    Sky so blue it makes you wonder
      If it's heaven shining through;
    Earth so smiling 'way out yonder,
      Sun so bright it dazzles you;
    Birds a-singing, flowers a-flinging
      All their fragrance on the breeze;
    Dancing shadows, green, still meadows—
      Don't you mope, you've still got these.

These, and none can take them from you;
　　These, and none can weigh their worth.
What! you're tired and broke and beaten?—
　　Why, you're rich—you've got the earth!
Yes, if you're a tramp in tatters,
　　While the blue sky bends above,
You've got nearly all that matters,
　　You've got God, and God is love.

PREMONITION

'Twas a year ago and the moon was bright
  (Oh, I remember so well, so well),
I walked with my love in a sea of light,
  And the voice of my sweet was a silver bell.

And sudden the moon grew strangely dull,
  And sudden my love had taken wing;
I looked on the face of a grinning skull,
  I strained to my heart a ghastly thing.

'Twas but fantasy, for my love lay still
  In my arms with her tender eyes aglow,
And she wondered why my lips were chill,
  Why I was silent and kissed her so.

A year has gone and the moon is bright,
  A gibbous moon like a ghost of woe:
I sit by a new-made grave to-night,
  And my heart is broken—it's strange, you
    know.

THE TRAMPS

Can you recall, dear comrade, when we tramped
    God's land together,
  And we sang the old, old Earth-song, for our
      youth was very sweet;
When we drank and fought and lusted, as we
    mocked at tie and tether,
  Along the road to Anywhere, the wide world
      at our feet.

Along the road to Anywhere, when each day had
    its story;
  When time was yet our vassal, and life's jest
      was still unstale;
When peace unfathomed filled our hearts as,
    bathed in amber glory,
  Along the road to Anywhere we watched the
      sunsets pale.

Alas! the road to Anywhere is pitfalled with
    disaster;

  There's hunger, want, and weariness, yet O we
      loved it so;

As on we tramped exultantly, and no man was
    our master,

  And no man guessed what dreams were ours,
      as swinging heel and toe,

We tramped the road to Anywhere, the magic
    road to Anywhere,

  The tragic road to Anywhere, such dear, dim
      years ago.

L'ENVOI

YOU who have lived in the Land,
*   You who have trusted the trail;*
You who are strong to withstand,
*   You who are swift to assail;*
Songs have I sung to beguile,
*   Vintage of desperate years*
Hard as a harlot's smile,
*   Bitter as unshed tears.*

Little of joy or mirth,
*   Little of ease I sing;*
Sagas of men of earth,
*   Humanly suffering,*
Such as you all have done;
*   Savagely faring forth,*
Sons of the midnight sun,
*   Argonauts of the North.*

124

Far in the land God forgot,
  Glimmers the lure of your trail ;
Still in your lust are you taught
  Even to win is to fail.
Still must you follow and fight,
  Under the vampire wing ;
There in the long, long night,
  Hoping and vanquishing.

      Husbandmen of the Wild,
        Reaping a barren gain ;
      Scourged by desire, reconciled
        Unto disaster and pain ;
      These my songs are for you,
        You who are seared with the brand,
      God knows I have tried to be true ;
        Please God you will understand.